Death Valley National Park is properly labeled the driest place in the United States. Yet water's past presence here is obvious... in the patterned mud flats exposed between dunes, in the ancient marine sediments that bound the valley. Spring wildflowers along a canyon floor are colorful proof of storms six months past. Hundreds of springs provide water for animals and people, and winter storms temporarily dust upper slopes with snow.

*T*he ever-changing landscape of illusion: dunes of sand are blown into undulating waves, which seem to lap at the Grapevine Mountains, much as the waters of glacial-era lakes did long ago.

Death Valley National Park, *located in eastern California and western Nevada, was first set aside in 1933 to preserve this unique desert that includes the lowest point in the Western Hemisphere.*

Front cover: Death Valley Dunes and Tucki Mountain, photo by Jeff Gnass. Inside front cover: Lonely tracks lead toward shaded mud cracks, photo by Dick Dietrich. Page 1: Yuccas below the Cottonwood Mountains, photo by Willard Clay. Pages 2/3: The Grapevine Mountains frame ever-shifting sand dunes, photo by Jeff Gnass. Pages 4/5: Dante's View in late afternoon, photo by Tom Algire.

Edited by Cheri C. Madison.
Book design by K. C. DenDooven.

Sixth Printing, 2002

in pictures DEATH VALLEY The Continuing Story
© 1989 KC PUBLICATIONS, INC.

*"The Story Behind the Scenery"; "in pictures... The Continuing Story";
the parallelogram forms and colors within are registered
in the U.S. Patent and Trademark Office.*

LC 89-80843. ISBN 0-88714-039-4.

in pictures
Death Valley
The Continuing Story®

by Kayci Cook

Kayci Cook grew up in several southwestern National Park Service areas before beginning her own NPS career. A graduate of Northern Arizona University with a degree in natural resources management, Kayci spent several years as a supervisory park ranger in Death Valley National Monument.

RAY ATKESON

*N*ational park areas are special landscapes set aside by acts of Congress to protect and preserve features of national significance that are generally categorized as scenic, scientific, historical and recreational.

As Americans, we are joint caretakers of these unique places, and we gladly share them with visitors from around the world.

"Death Valley" — the name implies desolation and lifelessness. Dun-colored badlands rise like ghosts from the valley floor; plants and animals seem altogether absent. Explore beyond these first impressions, and you will find the valley's deadly reputation to be largely undeserved. Native Americans have called this place home for at least 10,000 years. Mountain canyons are green with grape and willow. Great blue herons circle above spring-fed pools filled with tiny fish that sparkle like silver dollars. Don't be fooled by Death Valley's facade, for her beauty is not at all lifeless.

The illusion of lifelessness reigns near Twenty Mule Team Canyon. Here mudstone badlands support little vegetation.

The Forces That Created Death Valley

Death Valley showcases many of the earth's physical processes. Rocks here represent a remarkably complete, if confusing, record of the area's geologic history. Exposed in the mountains are ocean sediments thousands of feet thick, in places baked and compressed into crystalline rocks. Past periods of mountain building bent and broke rock layers into crazy patterns and thrust once-buried formations into the light of day. Volcanoes spewed ash and oozed lava over the landscape. Faults broke the crust into blocks that rotated mountains up, basins down. In wetter times, the wind-driven waves of a deep lake cut shorelines into rock 600 feet above the basin floor. Death Valley is a product of our dynamic earth and, accordingly, the view that seems so timeless to us is bound to change. Mountains will disintegrate; canyons will widen. Faults may raise new mountains, and volcanoes may fill the silent desert air with deafening sound once more.

△ **Titus Canyon, slicing through the Grapevine Mountains, gives a glimpse of several** chapters in Death Valley's geologic story. A one-way, high-clearance gravel road travels 26 miles from the park's eastern boundary to the Scotty's Castle road. Near Red Pass, look for pinnacle-like volcanic plugs. In Titus Canyon note where forces bent once-level strata into wide folds, long before faulting and erosion exposed their graceful lines.

TOM BEAN

△ **Under extremely high**
temperature and pressure,
even solid rock will flow.
Compression contorted these
layers in Red Wall Canyon into
tight accordion folds. This
pattern is repeated throughout
the Grapevine Mountains.

JEFF GNASS

On a small scale, even ▷
plants contribute to the widening
of desert canyons. In Titus
Canyon the greater forces of
faulting and flash flooding create
crevices where hardy plants can
get a foothold. As they grow, their
roots exert pressures and may
produce weak acids that further
crumble the rock.

A Wearing Away of Rock

△ **From Aguereberry Point, high in the** Panamint Range, the scene seems static, unchanging. This sense of permanence is false, however. Mountains raised to prominence by crustal movements become immediately vulnerable to the powers of erosion that will ultimately bring them down again. With the next storm these rocks may begin their unavoidable journey toward the valley.

△ **Even the hardest rock is not** immune to the agents of weathering. As you wander the serpentine channel of Mosaic Canyon, consider the forces that carve and polish these marble walls with each new storm. Water and debris from far up-canyon are funneled through this narrow slot before fanning out at the canyon's mouth. Gravels stranded high above the canyon floor remind us of the flood's fury, now spent.

△ **N**ear Golden Canyon the agent of erosion has left a calling card: a spring carpet of
desertgold flowers. Water, unable to penetrate the clay-rich badlands, spreads out into the loose
gravels and cobbles of an alluvial fan where it becomes available to desert plants.

LARRY ULRICH

FRED HIRSCHMANN

△ **D**eath Valley rains are an infrequent but significant agent of landscape change. In spring or summer, a dramatic thunderstorm may last only minutes; but since most canyons drain huge areas, the effect may be great. Granite boulders too heavy to lift can be found in the lower reaches of Cottonwood Canyon, miles from their source.

JEFF GNASS

◁ **T**he episodic nature of dry-land erosion has produced some unusual landforms. Spanning Natural Bridge Canyon, the natural bridge was formed by a changing streamcourse. From its original course, the stream took a bend to the north (left), but later reverted to the straighter path. With each flash flood, erosion undercut the rock, eventually leaving a bridge above the canyon floor.

The Force of Water

JEFF GNASS

JOHN DITTLI

△ **When the Black Mountains were** uplifted, these ancient alluvial fan deposits in Furnace Creek Wash were dragged along and tilted up at crazy angles. Gravity and water will eventually level these "fanglomerates," and the process will begin anew as gravels spread out like aprons around the mountains.

◁ **Red Cathedral, visible** from the Golden Canyon trail, reminds one of the cyclic nature of mountain building and erosion. Now standing above its own alluvial fan, Red Cathedral is composed of cemented gravels eroded from another mountain range, long since dispatched by the forces of weathering.

13

Forces of Nature

◁ **Just a few thousand** years ago, the valley's silence was shattered by volcanic explosions. The most recent of these created Ubehebe Crater, one-half mile wide and 700 feet deep. Molten material rising toward the surface met with underground water. Heat instantly turned water to steam, blasting away the overlying rock layers and blanketing the area with cinders. To appreciate Ubehebe's scale, hike along the rim or walk into the crater itself.

K.C. DENDOOVEN

◁ **An aerial view of** The Racetrack reveals the unique characteristics of a desert playa, or saline lake. Faults on both sides of the basin lowered it relative to the mountains on each edge. As erosion brought down rocks from the higher points, alluvial fans grew outward from the mountains and finally merged at the basin's center. Playas are the most level of all earth's topographic surfaces. Here rain or snow can leave a temporary lake covering acres, only inches deep.

LEWIS KEMPER—DRK PHOTO

△ **Grooves in the now dry playa surface chronicle the** travels of boulders across the basin. The mechanism for this mysterious phenomenon still eludes geologists. Presumably, weather and geology combine to set the rocks in motion. When wet, the playa is quite slick; stones that have fallen onto the playa from a nearby cliff may be ferried by strong winds along the slippery surface. Winds can change the direction of rock travel as zigzag trails suggest.

CARR CLIFTON

Sun, Salt, and Water

△ **In a place notoriously dry, many visitors** are surprised to learn that water is often inches below their feet. Death Valley's topography has made it a vast sump, a final resting spot for much of the region's groundwater. Underground faults guide water inexorably toward Death Valley, where hundreds of springs and seeps mark its journey's end. One of the larger water bodies, Salt Creek swells to a respectable stream during the cool months of winter and early spring. Summer temperatures shrink the stream back to its source pools. Such surface evaporation is the fate of most water in Death Valley.

Salt pinnacles mantled with silt at Devils ▷ Golf Course impart a third dimension to the otherwise flat basin floor. Water flowing into the valley brings dissolved material from nearby rock formations. These materials recombine into various salts—carbonates, sulfates, and chlorides—according to available chemicals. When concentrations reach critical levels, salts crystallize out of their solutions and form a crust where water evaporates. This crust of sodium chloride, little different from table salt, is continually sculpted by wind and rain.

Life in the Sun

The national park's 3.3 million acres of varied landforms are home to a surprising diversity of living things, a native flora and fauna with contributions from both the Mojave and Great Basin deserts. Though the notion of life here appears unthinkable at first, the area's subtle ecosystem manifests, yet again, Death Valley's illusory nature. Life here is at once predictable and erratic, conspicuous and obscure. An underlying order is suggested by the regular spacing of creosote bush and the methodical change in vegetation from salt pan to mountain peak. In contrast, the erratic nature of desert storms and the wildflower displays dependent upon them illustrate randomness and chance. Large mammals such as the ever-present coyote and the majestic bighorn overshadow the valley's smaller inhabitants, the tiny pupfish and springsnails of area pools and seeps. All are bound together by a dependence on that most valued of desert commodities: water.

FRANK S. BALTHIS

△ **Like all creatures, a roadrunner requires** food, water, shelter and space for survival. Although they can fly, roadrunners prefer to chase down their prey, feeding on insects, lizards and snakes. Water can be hard to get and easy to lose. Moist prey may supplement drinking water, but cooling behaviors like panting can be costly as water is lost to the dry air. Shelter is found under trees and shrubs, and space is, of course, plentiful.

▷ **Rivaling colorful rock formations along** Artists Drive, calthaleaf phacelias blanket alluvial fans with vivid purple. When rains are unusually frequent and well-timed throughout the season, seeds lying dormant for years can explode into a spectacular, if short-lived, display. Death Valley's wildflowers are as ephemeral as the rains they rely on.

A Land of Extremes

TOM BEAN

FRED HIRSCHMANN

△ **Death Valley's mountains sport a** *reverse tree line—only above the line is there moisture enough to support trees. High in the Panamints, bristlecone pines guard the slopes of Telescope Peak. These trees may be thousands of years old. How can they live so long? Some researchers suggest that adversity begets longevity. For example, the cold climate discourages the spread of wildfire and the growth of microorganisms, both of which would otherwise be life threatening.*

△ **Green ephedra, growing on the upper** *slopes of Marble Peak, appears at first to have no leaves. Yet the green jointed stems do support leaves which have evolved into tiny scales, barely visible. Also known as Mormon tea, ephedras are non-flowering plants or gymnosperms, like pines and other conifers. They reproduce when pollen from small male cones reaches a female cone, usually on a separate plant.*

20

RUSS FINLEY

△ **Hummocky stands of arrowweed form the Devils Cornfield. The same force which** shapes nearby sand dunes fashions these salt-tolerant plants into "cornshocks." Their roots exposed by scouring winds, arrowweed plants still grow, leaving below a shaggy snarl of old roots and branches.

BILL RATCLIFFE

△ **Heralding the heat, desert four o'clock** flowers open in late afternoon, the hottest part of the day.

JEFF GNASS

A study in interdependence, the Joshua tree ▷ relies on a single insect, the pronuba moth, to pollinate its creamy blossoms.

Life on the Wing

LARRY BURTON

◁ **Look for Gambel's quail near permanent water** sources throughout the valley. Traveling in groups, or coveys, they confuse predators and startle hikers by exploding from the brush into flapping flight.

LARRY BURTON

△ **Identify this hawk on the wing by its** fan-shaped tail, crimson when backlighted by the sun. Red-tailed hawks hunt by day, soaring on rising air currents in search of prey.

NPS PHOTO BY ROSALIE ANNE LA RUE

△ **A checkerspot butterfly, bright against the** desert pavement, pauses in its quest for nectar. Death Valley is home to a surprising variety of moths and butterflies.

△ **Look again. The small** ▷ shape hovering above spring flowers, its wings blurred in rapid motion, is not a bird but a moth—the white-lined sphinx. Appropriately, these insects are also known as hummingbird moths. Wings whir furiously as they drink nectar through tube-like mouthparts unrolled into the flower. This style of flight is energy consumptive so the sphinx chooses only flowers with a high sugar content. Rapid wingbeats also produce excess body heat that the sphinx must dissipate. Regurgitating water droplets onto its body, the moth is cooled by evaporation. White-lined sphinx moths play a key role in plant survival as their journeys serve to pollinate flowers.

The Living Desert

▽ **Chuckwallas eat only plants,** despite their fierce appearance. They live among boulders, well camouflaged by mottled skin.

FRANK S. BALTHIS

FRANK S. BALTHIS

△ **From moist foods eaten in spring,** a desert tortoise can store a cup of water in its bladder for later metabolic use. Desert tortoises have been listed as an endangered species. Facing increasing habitat loss elsewhere in their range, they find a haven in places like Death Valley and Joshua Tree national parks.

Shockley goldenhead is a ▷ perennial plant, persisting on upper slopes throughout the year. Flowering is timed according to rainfall and may occur twice each year. The first bloom is in spring, golden flowers contrasting sharply with rocky hillsides. Slopes may burst into color again in response to summer thundershowers. Beyond mere decoration, in wet years Death Valley's flowering plants provide many desert-dwelling animals with additional forage.

◁ **Preceding pages: Long ago** covered by the waters of an ancient lake, Manly Beacon is bathed in the golden light of a desert sunrise. Photo by Tom Algire.

The majestic curved ▷
horns of the desert bighorn
ram are not only elegant,
but functional. During the
breeding season rams
compete for females by
butting heads; the
thickened bony core of the
horn and thickened base of
the skull protect the ram
from injury during such
contests. To the victor, the
dominant male, belong the
spoils of mating.

BILL RATCLIFFE

△ **Search the dunes for hook-shaped tracks of sidewinders,**
active mainly at night. Their sideways travel is
well-suited to loose sand.

BILL RATCLIFFE

DIANE ALLEN

Living life on the run, a suspicious jackrabbit pauses ▷
between mouthfuls to sniff the air. Acute senses and an
explosive, evasive run toward cover make the jackrabbit
easy to spot, but hard to catch.

Of Birds and Flowers

CARR CLIFTON

△ **T**racks in the sand may lead only to questions...what was this bird in search of?

DAVID MUENCH

Beavertail cacti seem to be marching toward the △ Funeral Mountains. Expect to see this variety of prickly-pear from alluvial fans to mountain peaks where moisture is at least seasonally available. Magenta flowers grace the wrinkled pads March through June, peaking in April.

Water here is scarce ▷
and competition for it fierce.
To meet their moisture needs,
plants are usually spaced
widely. Creosote bushes have
roots that exude a growth
inhibitor which keeps
neighbors at a safe distance.
At the mouth of a canyon,
more abundant water
loosens space requirements
between desert rocknettle
and desert holly.

◁ **D**eath Valley gilmania or goldcarpet is
low growing, as the name implies. A rare and
endemic plant, it is found nowhere
else in the world.

△ **D**esert fivespots are among the most
popular wildflowers with visitors and, in
this case, a tiny spider.

◁ **T**he delicate yellow flowers of Death Valley
mojavea dot alluvial fans in spring.

*◁ **E**arly travelers* in Death Valley had to be resourceful. This wagon seems to be made of another's spare parts—probably from whatever bits and pieces the miners could scrounge.

***Successful** ▷* prospectors combined skill, luck, and a good head for business. In 1904, Jack Keane and his partner discovered a small silver-lead prospect and then, accidentally, a ledge rich in free gold. The Keane Wonder Mine, high in the Funeral Mountains, became one of the area's most productive. The partners eventually sold their interests for $50,000 plus stock.

Death Valley's Early Days

In 1849, the lure of gold in the Sierra Nevada brought the first pioneers accidentally into Death Valley. Not realizing the mineral wealth that lay before their eyes and beneath their feet, they traveled on, leaving the valley's riches for later fortune-seekers. By the 1870s, prospectors combed the hills. Strikes were made, and fortunes won and lost as glittering ledges of ore gave out. First overlooked as worthless salt, soon borax sparked a boom of its own. Not surprisingly, transportation was a common problem for most early travelers and residents. High mountains enclose the valley on nearly all sides, and there were few dependable roads until improvement began in the 1920s and '30s by individuals and later the National Park Service.

NPS PHOTO

△ **In the 1920s, few roads led to Death Valley. Bob** Eichbaum, intending to build a resort hotel at Stovepipe Wells, realized that access was critical. Petitioning the county, he received permission to build a toll road from the Panamint Valley, over Towne Pass, to Stovepipe Wells. In 1926, fees for the Mt. Whitney toll road were $1 per animal and $2 per automobile—occupants paid 50¢ extra.

NPS PHOTO

◁ **Prospectors** relied on burros to pack supplies across rugged desert terrain. The donkey became a symbol of the "single-blanket jackass prospector." As prospecting played out, burros were left to run wild and reproduced rapidly. Their large numbers soon impacted springs, vegetation, and wildlife. The National Park Service now works to control their numbers.

△ *The "twenty mule team" slogan created for advertising, actually depicted teams consisting* of 18 mules and 2 horses. The horses were hitched closest to the wagon tongue to enable their greater weight to aid in maneuvering the huge wagons. To carry loads of borax to the nearest railhead, the teams had to negotiate tight turns, deep sand, and steep grades.

*Both Death Valley ▷
National Monument and
the Civilian Conservation
Corps (CCC) were
created in 1933. With no
funds for a monument
staff, two CCC camps
were created in Death
Valley to begin
development. CCC
workers built over 500
miles of roads, with 175 of
those paved. They also
operated a greenhouse,
and made adobe bricks
for construction. Many
buildings from this era are
still in use today.*

*T*he valley's best-known prospector was "Death △ ▷
Valley Scotty." Walter Scott's long association with Death
Valley began with his first visit in the 1800s. Returning later
to prospect, Scott ultimately met and joined in with Albert
Johnson (top photo), who financed his mining ventures. Their
business partnership culminated in a lifelong friendship
and the building of "Scotty's Castle," Johnson's vacation
home. Scotty also witnessed creation of Death Valley
National Monument in 1933, and conferred with the first
superintendent, Col. John R. White (right photo).

◁ *D*uring the early
years, National Park
Service staff at Death
Valley National
Monument followed the
example of local
Timbisha people by
seasonally migrating
into the mountains. In
summer, monument
operations were moved
from the heat of the
valley floor into the
cooler confines of
Wildrose Canyon.

Death Valley: The Human Experience

Death Valley has both attracted and repulsed people for millennia. Native Americans camped here on the shores of Lake Manly 10,000 years ago. Later, Shoshone would leave the unforgiving summer heat of the valley floor for cooler mountain camps. The first documented Anglo visitors suffered incredible hardships and are credited with giving the valley its frightful name. Even so, several returned to search for riches. Activity and silence alternated with the boom and bust cycles of mining: gold, silver, lead, copper, borax.

"Single-blanket jackass prospectors" led their burros up rocky canyons, while teamsters drove twenty-mule-team wagons across the shimmering salt pan. Other visitors documented low points, high temperatures, state boundaries, and biological specimens. By 1920, people began to come for yet another reason—to see for themselves this mysterious place. They came by horse and wagon, and later by train and car. And still they come, park visitors, to a place rich in life, in color, in human history. They come to Death Valley.

▽ *The Badwater basin is justly famous as the lowest spot in the Western Hemisphere. From here the formidable salt pan stretches to meet the distant Panamint Mountains. Nowhere else in Death Valley is the vertical relief so evident. Visitors are immediately confronted by a strange pool of water; spring-fed and more brackish than the sea, it seems devoid of life. Hidden among the pickleweed plants is the peculiar Badwater snail, so small its shell is measured in millimeters. Years of pedestrian trampling have destroyed much of its habitat, the fragile salt crustal roof on the pool's margin. Tread lightly.*

CARLOS ELMER

RAY ATKESON

△ **A**t dawn and dusk, undulating dunes issue a colorful invitation to add your tracks to those of the wind. Make your own trail as one crest line dissolves into another. The Mesquite Flat dune field covers 15 square miles and is accessible by foot from its eastern and southwestern margins. Carry water, wear a hat, and note where you have parked.

Early Visitors and Residents

The discovery of gold in ▷
California set wagon wheels from
all over America in motion as
fortune-seeking emigrants headed
west. Several such groups
blundered into Death Valley late in
1849, lured off the Spanish Trail by
a crude map showing a shortcut to
the gold fields. All but one group
had to abandon their wagons, as
well as most of their belongings,
often slaughtering their oxen for
food as they attempted to escape
the rugged terrain. In an annual
reenactment of the first pioneer
crossing, wagons traverse
the desert.

DEANNA DULEN

DEANNA DULEN

△ **R**ubber-tired wagons remind us that this is the twentieth century. These modern
pioneers are participants in the annual Death Valley '49er Encampment held each November to
commemorate the historic 1849 crossing. Other encampment activities include a fiddlers' contest
and a western art show.

GAIL BANDINI

FRANK S. BALTHIS

⚠ *A far cry from an air-conditioned* automobile, the Panamint Valley Stage on display at the Borax Museum ran between Skidoo in the Panamint Mountains and the Rhyolite and Beatty area in Nevada in 1907.

⚠ *Even experienced desert residents fell* prey to the valley's extremes. Mesquites shade the graves of James Dayton and Shorty Harris. After years of surviving Death Valley weather, Dayton and his team of mules died of exposure less than 20 miles from Furnace Creek Ranch. Harris, a well-known prospector, did not die in Death Valley, but requested burial beside his friend Dayton.

△ **Mining ruins at Leadfield in Titus Canyon crouch beneath upended rock layers.**
*Prospectors looked for such vertical outcrops in search of ore-bearing quartz veins. If the
concentration of ore was high enough, shafts or tunnels were excavated to meet and follow the vein.
The boom that started Leadfield began in 1905 but soon fizzled because of transportation problems.
Renewed interest during the 1920s resulted in establishment of the town and building
of the Titus Canyon road.*

The Mining Era

Long a symbol of ▷
Death Valley, this twenty-mule-team wagon at Harmony Borax Works was designed specifically to haul borax from here to the railhead at Mojave, 165 miles away. Total load weight pulled by the teams (actually 18 mules and 2 horses) was over 30 tons.

RUSS FINLEY

JEFF GNASS

△ **Still smelling of charred wood, charcoal kilns now stand cold and silent in Wildrose** Canyon. From 1877-78 the woods rang with the sound of axes as pinyon trees were felled and fired in the stone kilns to produce charcoal. The charcoal was then hauled west across Panamint Valley to fire silver smelters in the Argus Mountains.

Trains, Trams, and Tailings

JEFF GNASS

◁ **T**he Keane Wonder Mine in the Funeral Mountains produced over $1 million in gold, making it one of the most successful mines in the region. Ore from the hillside mines was transported to a stamp mill below by a tram system. Gravity drew filled ore buckets downward along stretched cables and pulled empty buckets back up to the top. Today the framing timbers of the lower terminal mark the end of the tramline.

Ruins of an office ▷ building and other foundations identify the site of Ashford Mill, visible from the Badwater road at the valley's southern end. Although the structures still standing date from the 1930s, Harold Ashford began working gold claims in the Black Mountains in 1907.

GAIL BANDINI

*T*he discovery of ▷ "cottonball" borax on the valley floor began the best-known chapter in Death Valley's mining history. In the 1880s, Chinese laborers scraped up mounds of borate salts taken by sled for processing at Harmony Borax Works. These borax windrows or "haystacks" date from later mining, to show development on patented claims. Periodic flooding will eventually reclaim the salty hummocks.

CHARLIE BORLAND

*S*ymbolic of the ▷ transition between borax mining and tourism, the Death Valley Railroad ran from Death Valley Junction to the town of Ryan. As the mines played out, this locomotive, now at the Borax Museum, carried less borax and more visitors.

CHARLIE BORLAND

JEFF GNASS

△ **Formally known as Death Valley Ranch, Scotty's Castle stands as a monument to an unlikely** friendship. Albert Johnson, a Chicago businessman, visited prospector Walter Scott in 1906 to check on the mine his money was grubstaking. His health improved by the weather and his sense of humor tickled by "Death Valley Scotty," Johnson and his wife Bessie later built these structures as a vacation home. Daily tours of Scotty's Castle illuminate their 1930s lifestyle.

FRED HIRSCHMANN

◁ **Enjoy this** oasis in Grapevine Canyon, beneath shady cottonwood trees. In such an atmosphere it is easy to imagine Scotty strolling over to tell a few outrageous stories of his days in the valley.

Scotty's Castle

FRED HIRSCHMANN

⟁ **"With perseverance we will** succeed" is the Latin motto borne by the Johnsons' made-to-order Italian flatware. The dishes also sport initials for Johnson, Scott, and Death Valley Ranch.

LARRY ULRICH

⟁ **A Howard clock on the chimes tower marks the passage** of time at Scotty's Castle. The Johnsons loved music and the 25-note set of Deagan chimes could be operated from the dining room, music room and the tower's second floor. One hopes that visitors staying in the tower's first floor guest apartment liked music as well.

FRED HIRSCHMANN

⟁ **The Johnsons' 1933 Packard coupe roadster was purchased new in** 1933 and brought to the castle in 1940. It contains a 12-cylinder engine and was considered one of the most powerful automobiles of its day.

RUSS FINLEY

△ **Centered about several freshwater springs, Furnace Creek is a green oasis of palms** *and mesquite trees. This is the largest area of human activity within Death Valley National Park, with several campgrounds, the Visitor Center, and Furnace Creek Inn and Ranch.*

Death Valley Natural History Association

The Death Valley Natural History Association supports the park in many ways. A private, non-profit organization, it was created to provide visitors with information to enhance their stay. Several sales outlets offer publications and other media about Death Valley; some of these books were published by the association. Proceeds from sales help fund yet other means of visitor enjoyment: the three-dimensional model of Death Valley on display in the Visitor Center and telescopes used by rangers in night sky programs.

SUGGESTED READING

BRYAN, T. SCOTT, and BETTY TUCKER-BRYAN. *The Explorer's Guide to Death Valley National Park.* Niwot: University of Colorado Press, 1995.

CLARK, BILL. *Death Valley: The Story Behind the Scenery.* Las Vegas, Nevada: KC Publications, Inc., rev. ed., 2002.

CORNETT, JAMES W. *Wildlife of North American Deserts.* Palm Springs, California: Nature Trails Press, 1987.

FERRIS, ROXANA S. *Wildflowers of Death Valley.* Bishop, California: Death Valley Natural History Association, 1983.

FIERO, BILL. *Geology of the Great Basin.* Reno, University of Nevada Press, 1986.

LINGENFELTER, RICHARD P. *Death Valley and the Amargosa.* Berkeley: University of California Press, 1986.

PAHER, STANLEY W. *Death Valley's Scotty's Castle: The Story Behind the Scenery.* Las Vegas, Nevada: KC Publications, 1985.

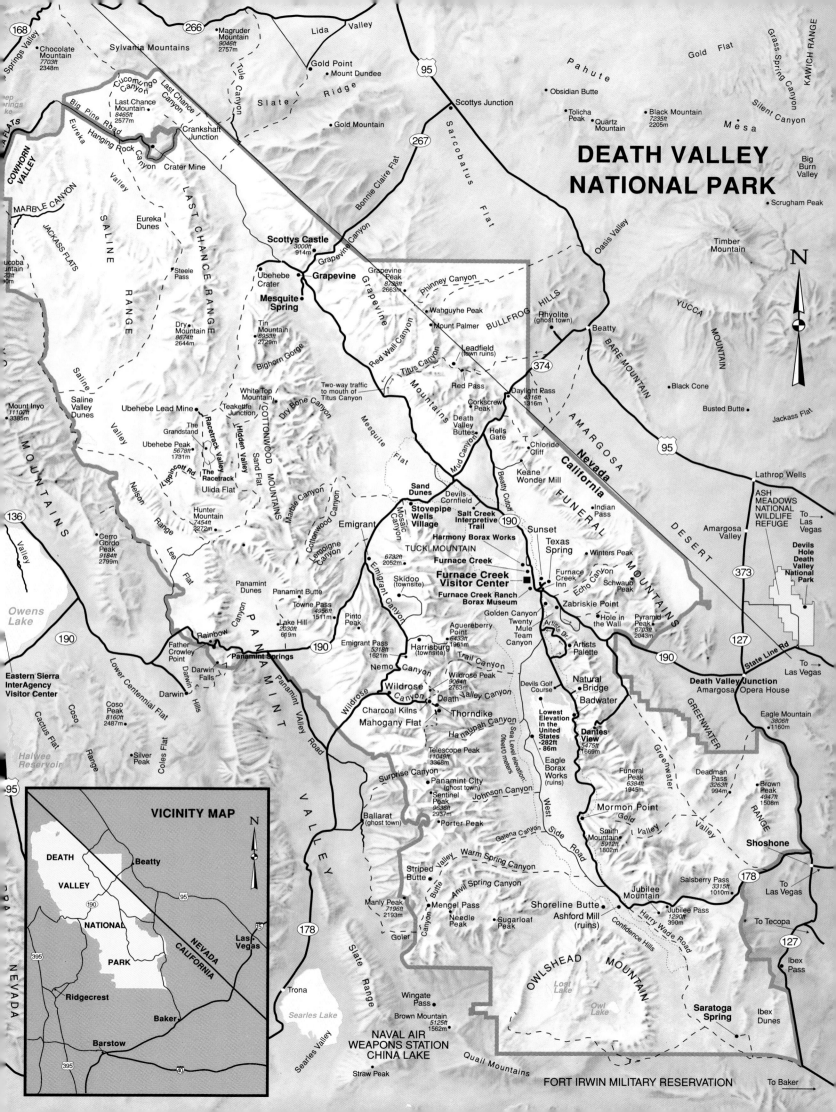

DICK DIETRICH

Grand desolation. From elevated vantage points, the mysterious valley, with its wrinkled foothills and glittering salt flats, appears to stretch beyond the horizon. Mountains rising abruptly from the valley floor etch a jagged outline against an azure sky. The scale here is impressive. By comparison, humans seem small and insignificant. Our impact on this ageless landscape, however, can be great. The desert, despite its hardy appearance, is a fragile place. Off-road vehicle tracks take years to heal, and vandalized archaeological sites will never reveal the full story of their occupants. We are all stewards of America's national parks, charged with their safekeeping. From Zabriskie Point or Dantes View, let the spectacular vista of a land more vulnerable than invincible remind us that continued existence of wild places like Death Valley National Park depends on our thoughtful actions.

A photographer catches first light on the hills near Zabriskie Point.

BILL RATCLIFFE

△ **E**lements as artists, sun, rain, and wind combine constantly to rearrange the desert's beauty. Nature's touch can be harsh, as in a sandstorm, or gentle. Almost invisible, the imprints of raindrops mark sun-baked mud cracks.

KC Publications has been the leading publisher of colorful, interpretive books about National Park areas, public lands, Indian lands, and related subjects for over 39 years. We have 6 active series—over 125 titles—with Translation Packages in up to 8 languages for over half the areas we cover. Write, call, or visit our web site for our full-color catalog.

Our series are:

The Story Behind the Scenery® – Compelling stories of over 65 National Park areas and similar Public Land areas. Some with Translation Packages.

in pictures... The Continuing Story® – A companion, pictorially oriented, series on America's National Parks. All titles have Translation Packages.

For Young Adventurers™ – Dedicated to young seekers and keepers of all things wild and sacred. Explore America's Heritage from A to Z.

Voyage of Discovery® – Exploration of the expansion of the western United States.

Indian Culture and the Southwest – All about Native Americans, past and present.

Calendars – For National Parks and Southwest Indian culture, in dramatic full color, and a companion Color Your Own series, with crayons.

To receive our full-color catalog featuring over 125 titles—Books, Calendars, Screen Scenes, Videos, Audio Tapes, and other related specialty products:

Call (800-626-9673), fax (702-433-3420), write to the address below, Or visit our web site at www.kcpublications.com

Published by KC Publications, 3245 E. Patrick Ln., Suite A, Las Vegas, NV 89120.

Inside back cover: Mud ▷ cracks create a jigsaw puzzle design at Mesquite Flat. Photo by Jeff Gnass.

Back cover: Altered layers ▷ of volcanic ash provide the paints at Artists Palette. Photo by Larry Ulrich.

Created, Designed, and Published in the U.S.A.
Printed by Tien Wah Press (Pte.) Ltd, Singapore